DAVID

Plays Hide-and-Seek in the City

Juega al Escondite en la Cuidad

by Dolores Mayorga

Translated from the Spanish
by Lori Ann Schatschneider

Lerner Publications Company • Minneapolis

This edition published 1992
by Lerner Publications Company
241 First Avenue North
Minneapolis, Minnesota 55401 USA

Originally published as *David juega al escondite en la ciudad*
by Editorial Planeta, S.A., Barcelona, Spain
© Dolores Mayorga, 1989

Translation copyright © 1992 by Lerner Publications Company
Translated from the Spanish by Lori Ann Schatschneider

Library of Congress Cataloging-in-Publication Data

Mayorga, Dolores.
    [David juega al escondite en la ciudad. English]
    David plays hide-and-seek in the city = David juega al
escondite en la ciudad / Dolores Mayorga ; translated
from the Spanish by Lori Ann Schatschneider.
        p.   cm.
    Summary: David, Mario the thief, and Alicia play hide-
and-seek throughout the city. The reader is invited to find
them and other named items in each illustration.
    ISBN 0-8225-2002-8
    [1. Hide-and-seek—Fiction. 2. Picture puzzles. 3. Spanish
language materials—Bilingual.] I. Title. II. Title: David
juega al escondite en la ciudad.
PZ73.M36   1992
[Fic]—dc20   91-44171
                                                 CIP
                                                  AC

Manufactured in the United States of America

1 2 3 4 5 6 7 8 9 10 01 00 99 98 97 96 95 94 93 92

David plays hide-and-seek at school, at home, and throughout the city. Mario the thief and Alicia, with her umbrella, also try to pass by unnoticed.

David juega al escondite en la escuela, en casa, y por toda la ciudad. Mario el ladrón y Alicia, con su paraguas, procuran pasar inadvertidos también.

David learns many
things at school.

*David aprende muchas
cosas en la escuela.*

••••••••••••••••••••••••••••••••••

David, Mario, and Alicia are
hiding. Can you find them and
these other things too?

*David, Mario, y Alicia se esconden.
¿Puedes encontrar a ellos y estas
otras cosas también?*

••••••••••••••••••••••••••••••••••

books
libros

drawings
dibujos

paintbrushes
brochas

doll
muñeca

bathroom
cuarto de baño

marbles
canicas

four teachers
cuatro maestros

two birds
dos pájaros

aprons
delantales

David goes shopping downtown.

David se va de compras al centro.

••••••••••••••••••••••••••••••

David, Mario, and Alicia are hiding. Can you find them and these other things too?

David, Mario, y Alicia se esconden. ¿Puedes encontrar a ellos y estas otras cosas también?

••••••••••••••••••••••••••••••

race car
coche de carreras

street map
plano

roller skates
patínes de ruedas

skis
esquís

baby
bebé

gift
regalo

swimsuit
traje de baño

stoplights
semáforos

bread
pan

On his way home, David crosses a busy square.

En camino a su casa, David cruza una plaza concurrida.

••••••••••••••••••••••••••••••••

David, Mario, and Alicia are hiding. Can you find them and these other things too?

David, Mario, y Alicia se esconden. ¿Puedes encontrar a ellos y estas otras cosas también?

••••••••••••••••••••••••••••••••

three motorcycles
tres motos

ten pigeons
diez palomas

two musicians
dos músicos

phone booth
cabina telefónica

streetlight
farola

twins
gemelas

clown
payaso

computer
computadora

black dog
perro negro

In David's neighborhood, the apartments are full of people.

En el barrio de David, los apartamentos están llenos de gente.

••••••••••••••••••••••••••

David, Mario, and Alicia are hiding. Can you find them and these other things too?

David, Mario, y Alicia se esconden. ¿Puedes encontrar a ellos y estas otras cosas también?

••••••••••••••••••••••••••

bathtub
bañera

mice
ratónes

hairbrush
cepillo

two candles
dos velas

painter
pintor

clock
reloj

fruit basket
cesta de fruta

tennis shoe
zapatilla

seven cats
siete gatos

David plays hide-and-seek with his friends in the park.

David juega al escondite con sus amigos en el parque.

◆◆◆◆◆◆◆◆◆◆◆◆◆◆◆◆◆◆◆◆◆◆◆

David, Mario, and Alicia are hiding. Can you find them and these other things too?

David, Mario, y Alicia se esconden. ¿Puedes encontrar a ellos y estas otras cosas también?

◆◆◆◆◆◆◆◆◆◆◆◆◆◆◆◆◆◆◆◆◆◆◆

three benches
tres bancos

fountains
fuentes

hose
manguera

newspaper
periódico

yellow pail
cubo amarillo

blue ball
balón azul

sandbox
arenal

slides
toboganes

swings
columpios

Even David does tricks at the circus.

Incluso David hace trucos en el circo.

◆◆◆◆◆◆◆◆◆◆◆◆◆◆◆◆◆◆◆◆◆◆◆

David, Mario, and Alicia are hiding. Can you find them and these other things too?

David, Mario, y Alicia se esconden. ¿Puedes encontrar a ellos y estas otras cosas también?

◆◆◆◆◆◆◆◆◆◆◆◆◆◆◆◆◆◆◆◆◆◆◆

magician
mago

trapeze
trapecio

three monkeys
tres monos

seal
foca

five elephants
cinco elefantes

four lions
cuatro leones

two horses
dos caballos

cannon
cañón

jugglers
malabaristas

David goes to the
market with his father.

*David se va al mercado
con su padre.*

◆◆◆◆◆◆◆◆◆◆◆◆◆◆◆◆◆◆◆◆◆◆◆◆◆◆◆◆◆

David, Mario, and Alicia are
hiding. Can you find them and
these other things too?

*David, Mario, y Alicia se esconden.
¿Puedes encontrar a ellos y estas
otras cosas también?*

◆◆◆◆◆◆◆◆◆◆◆◆◆◆◆◆◆◆◆◆◆◆◆◆◆◆◆◆◆

fishing pole
caña de pescar

eight scales
ocho balanzas

pineapples
piñas

sweeper
barrendero

knife
cuchillo

sausages
salchichas

strawberries
fresas

hat with fruit
sombrero con fruta

brown eggs
huevos morenos

David loves the amusement park!

¡A David le encanta el parque de atracciones!

••••••••••••••••••••••••••••••

David, Mario, and Alicia are hiding. Can you find them and these other things too?

David, Mario, y Alicia se esconden. ¿Puedes encontrar a ellos y estas otras cosas también?

••••••••••••••••••••••••••••••

bear
oso

witch
bruja

skier
esquiador

ice cream cones
helados

popcorn
palomitas

bell
campana

mountain climber
escalador

train
tren

ticket window
ventanilla

David thinks this is a strange soccer game.

David encuentra muy raro este partido de fútbol.

◆◆◆◆◆◆◆◆◆◆◆◆◆◆◆◆◆◆◆◆◆◆◆◆◆◆

David, Mario, and Alicia are hiding. Can you find them and these other things too?

David, Mario, y Alicia se esconden. ¿Puedes encontrar a ellos y estas otras cosas también?

◆◆◆◆◆◆◆◆◆◆◆◆◆◆◆◆◆◆◆◆◆◆◆◆◆◆

hens
gallinas

goalkeeper
portero

butterfly
mariposa

referee
árbitro

megaphone
megáfono

mole
topo

red flag
bandera roja

t.v. camera
tomavistas

tennis player
tenista

David likes to see all
the animals at the zoo.

*A David le gusta ver
todos los animales
en el zoo.*

••••••••••••••••••••••••••••

David, Mario, and Alicia are
hiding. Can you find them and
these other things too?

*David, Mario, y Alicia se esconden.
¿Puedes encontrar a ellos y estas
otras cosas también?*

••••••••••••••••••••••••••••

two giraffes
dos jirafas

diver
buzo

three flamingos
tres flamencos

donkey
burro

six mountain goats
seis cabras monteses

two camels
dos camellos

turtle
tortuga

seven palm trees
siete palmeras

two hippopotamuses
dos hipopótamos

About the Author and Illustrator
Dolores Mayorga lives in Barcelona, Spain, with
her husband and three children, where she writes and
illustrates children's books. Her favorite spot in the city is
the zoo. She loves animals, and had dogs, horses, and cows
as a child in Argentina.

Sobre la Autora y Artisa
*Dolores Mayorga vive en Barcelona, España, con su esposo
y sus tres hijos, donde escribe y ilustra libros para niños.
Su sitio favorito en la ciudad es el zoo. Le encantan
los animales, y tenía perros, caballos, y vacas
de joven en Argentina.*